This edition published by Parragon Books Ltd in 2015 and distributed by

Parragon Inc.
440 Park Avenue South, 13th Floor
New York, NY 10016
www.parragon.com

Written and retold by Rachel Elliot, Anne Marie Ryan, Steve Smallman, Ronne Randall
Illustrated by Nicola Evans, Jaime Temairik, Natalie and Tamsin Hinrichsen, Russell Julian
Edited by Rebecca Wilson
Cover illustrated by Victoria Assanelli

Every effort has been made to acknowledge the contributors to this book.
If we have made any errors, we will be pleased to rectify them in future editions.

ISBN 978-1-4723-5465-5

Printed in China

A Collection of
Stories for
3
Year Olds

PaRragon

Bath · New York · Cologne · Melbourne · Delhi
Hong Kong · Shenzhen · Singapore · Amsterdam

Contents

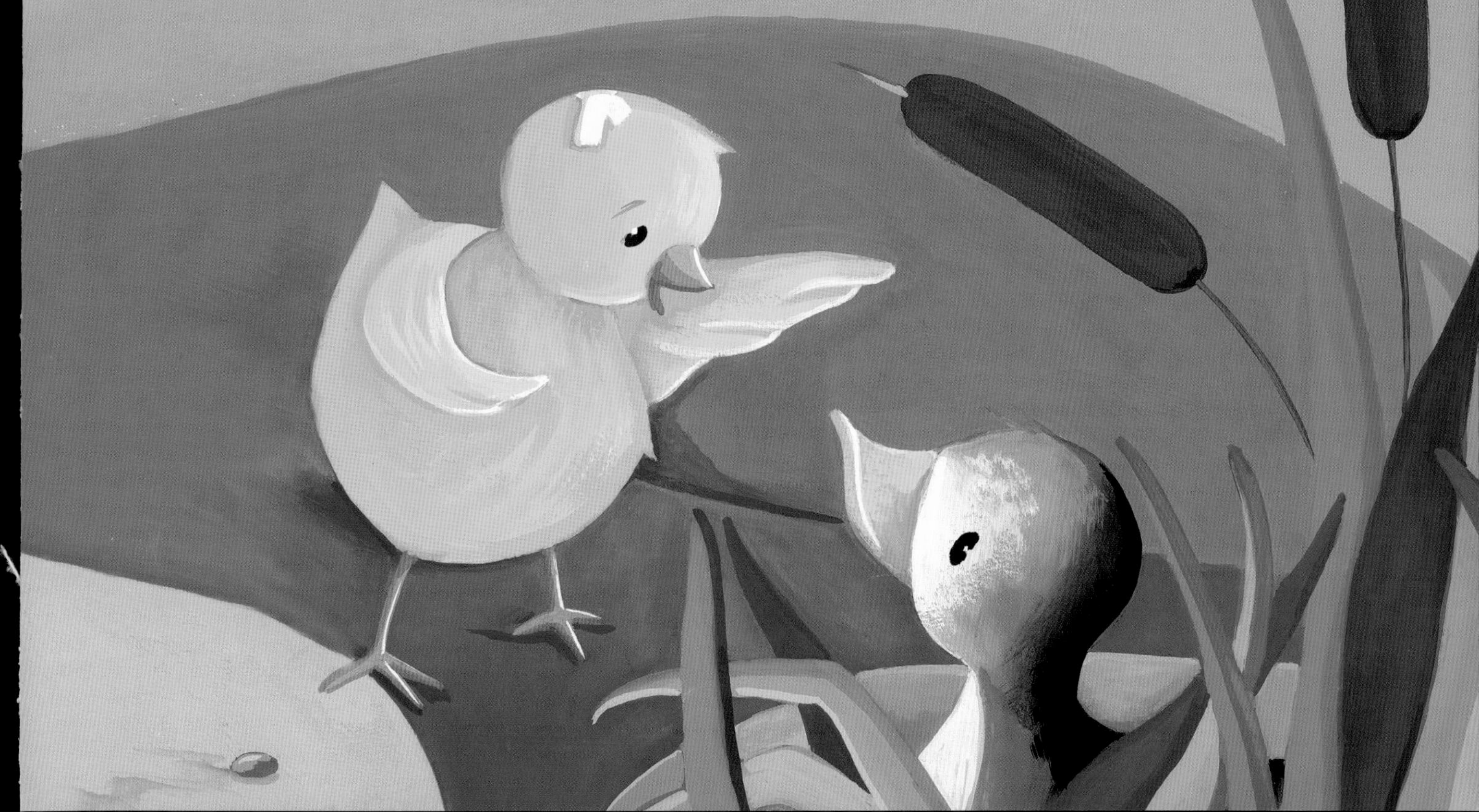

Chicken Little

One day, Chicken Little was walking down the road when ...

THWACK!

An acorn fell on his head!

"Ouch!" said Chicken Little, rubbing his head.

"I think the sky is falling! I must run and tell the king!"

So Chicken Little ran down the road to tell the king.
And on his way, he met Henny Penny.

"Where are you going in such a hurry?"

Henny Penny asked Chicken Little.

"The sky is falling, and I am
going to tell the king!" said
Chicken Little.

"I will come with you," said Henny Penny.

So Henny Penny and Chicken Little
rushed down the road. And on their way, they
met Cocky Locky.

"Where are you going in such a hurry?"

Cocky Locky asked them.

"The sky is falling, and we are going to tell
the king!" said Chicken Little.

"I will come with you," said Cocky Locky.

So Cocky Locky, Henny Penny, and Chicken Little dashed down the road. And on their way, they met Ducky Lucky.

"Where are you going in such a hurry?"

Ducky Lucky asked them.
"The sky is falling, and we are going to tell the king," said Chicken Little.
"I will come with you," said Ducky Lucky.

So Ducky Lucky,

Cocky Locky,

Henny Penny,

and Chicken Little

scurried down the road. And on their way, they met
Drakey Lakey.

"Where are you going in such a hurry?"

Drakey Lakey asked.

"The sky is falling, and we are going to tell the king," said Chicken Little.

"I will come with you," said Drakey Lakey.

So Drakey Lakey, Ducky Lucky,
Cocky Locky, Henny Penny, and Chicken Little
scampered down the road. And on their way, they
met Goosey Loosey.

"Where are you going in such a hurry?"

Goosey Loosey asked.
  "The sky is falling, and we are going to tell the king," said Chicken Little.

"I will come with you," said Goosey Loosey.

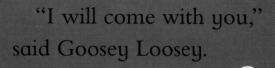

So Goosey Loosey, Drakey Lakey, Ducky Lucky, Cocky Locky, Henny Penny, and Chicken Little hurried down the road. And on their way, they met Turkey Lurkey.

"Where are you going in such a hurry?"

asked Turkey Lurkey.
    "The sky is falling, and we are going to tell the king," said Chicken Little.
    "I will come with you," said Turkey Lurkey.

So Turkey Lurkey, Goosey Loosey,
Drakey Lakey, Ducky Lucky, Cocky Locky,
Henny Penny, and Chicken Little raced
down the road. And on their way, they met
Foxy Loxy.

"Why, good day, my friends!" said Foxy Loxy. "And where might you all be going on this fine morning?"

"The sky is falling," said Chicken Little. "We are going to tell the king!"

"Really? How interesting. Have you ever been to the king's palace before?" asked Foxy Loxy.

"No," said Chicken Little. The others all shook their heads.

"Then how do you know you will find the way?" asked Foxy Loxy.

"Oh … I never thought of that," said Chicken Little.

"Why don't you let me help you?" said Foxy Loxy. "I know the way to the king's palace very well. Follow me, and you will be there in no time!"

So Chicken Little, Henny Penny, Cocky Locky, Ducky Lucky, Drakey Lakey, Goosey Loosey, and Turkey Lurkey all followed Foxy Loxy down the road.

Soon they came to a path that led into the woods.

They followed Foxy Loxy down the path …

into the woods …

...and straight to Foxy Loxy's den!

Foxy Loxy's wife and babies were waiting there, all ready to gobble up Chicken Little, Henny Penny, Cocky Locky, Ducky Lucky, Drakey Lakey, Goosey Loosey, and Turkey Lurkey!

So Turkey Lurkey, Goosey Loosey, Drakey Lakey, Ducky Lucky, Cocky Locky, Henny Penny, and Chicken Little all ran and flapped and flew away as fast as they could!

And they never did get
to tell the king that the sky
was falling.

Troll ... Two ... Three ... Four ...

Trolls like to laze about
twiddling their toes,
Picking their noses, and
having a doze.

They love to creep up
behind goats and go,

"BOO!"

Except for one sad, lonely troll:
Boogaloo.

The other trolls tried but could not understand
Why Boogaloo felt so alone in Troll Land.
"All I want is a friend," he thought with a sigh,
And just then, a shiny red THING floated by!

He ran after the thing and was running so fast,
He went straight by the sign that

NO
TROLL
SHOULD
GO PAST!

A second troll followed
behind Boogaloo,
Thinking, "Where is he going?
I want to go, too!"

They walked through the KEEP-OUT clouds straight to a place
Where a HUMAN BEING stood with a very shocked face.
The human being screamed, "I SEE TROLLS!" very loud,
And fled as a third troll came out of the cloud.

Another troll—number four—followed them, too,
Marching in line right behind Boogaloo.

And before you could say,

"boogie-boo!"

there were crowds
Of curious trolls popping out
through the clouds.

Trolls foul and furry were marching along,
Singing their favorite
troll marching song ...

"Troll, two, three, four ...

We're the trolls who grunt and snore.

Troll, two, three, four ...

We don't know, there might be more,

But we can only count to

fouuuuurrrr!"

The humans were frightened—
the trolls looked so scary,

So scruffy and smelly, so horrid and hairy!

As the trolls passed a park, Boogaloo snuck away.
He opened the gate, and he ran in to play!

"Hello," said a boy, "my name's Jake. Who are you?"
The little troll smiled and said,

"Boogaloo!"

"Come play on this whizz-thing!"
Boogaloo cried.
"All right," answered Jake.
"But we call it a slide!"

"Will you be my very best friend, Boogaloo?"
"Yes please!" the troll answered.
"Will you be mine, too?"
And Humans and Trolls all crept closer to see
What very best friends Trolls and Humans could be.

There is nothing between Trolls and Humans today:
The signs all came down, the clouds drifted away.
Together they play with balloons and toy boats,
And no one is frightened ...

... not even

the goats!

Rapunzel

Once upon a time, a poor young man and his wife lived next to an old witch.

The witch grew many vegetables in her garden.

One day, the man and his wife had nothing left to eat.

"Surely the witch won't notice if we took just a few carrots and cabbages," said the man to his wife.

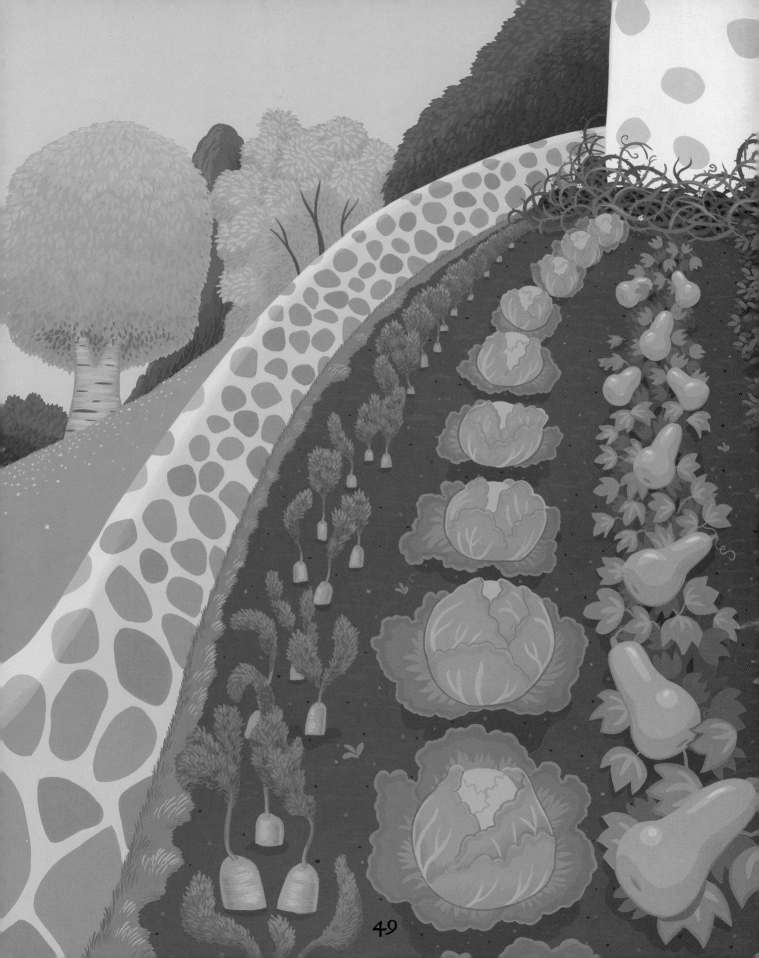

So the man quickly filled his basket. Suddenly, he heard an angry voice.

"Who said you could take MY vegetables?"

It was the old witch!

"Please don't hurt us," begged the man. "My wife is going to have a baby!"

"I will let you go," said the witch, "but you must give me the baby when it is born. I will care for it as my own."

The man was so scared, he agreed to everything the witch asked.

Soon, the man's wife had a baby girl. The very next day, the witch took the baby away.

The witch named the baby Rapunzel.

Rapunzel grew into a tall, beautiful girl with long, golden locks.

The witch was afraid that someone might take her away. So she locked her in a room at the top of a tower.

Each day, Rapunzel brushed her hair and gazed out of the window.

She sang sad, sweet songs to herself,

"How I wish the witch would set me free. There's a great big world I long to see."

One day, a prince was riding
in the forest. He heard Rapunzel's
beautiful singing and hid behind
a bush to listen.

Soon the witch arrived at the bottom of the
tower and called out,

"Rapunzel, Rapunzel,
let down your hair."

So Rapunzel
let down her long,
golden hair for the
witch to climb up.

The next day, the prince watched the witch slide down Rapunzel's hair. When she was far away, the prince called,

"Rapunzel, Rapunzel, let down your hair."

Down tumbled the
long, golden hair, and up
climbed the prince.

At first, Rapunzel was frightened of the stranger.
But they quickly became friends.

Rapunzel loved hearing the prince's stories.

He told her how it felt to run barefoot in a grassy meadow ...

... and how it felt to swim in the cold, blue sea.

Rapunzel had never seen such things!

"I will help you escape from the tower," promised the prince."

The prince visited Rapunzel whenever the witch went out. Every time, he would call out,

"Rapunzel, Rapunzel, let down your hair."

He brought silk string for Rapunzel to weave into a ladder. When it was long enough, Rapunzel planned to climb down the tower and escape.

Rapunzel worked on the ladder in secret. Soon, it nearly reached the ground.

One day, Rapunzel forgot
about her secret.

"You are much heavier than
the prince," she told the witch.

The old witch was very angry.

She grabbed the scissors from Rapunzel's sewing basket
and cut up the ladder.

SNIP!   SNIP!   SNIP!

Then she cut off Rapunzel's hair
and cast a spell.
   Poor Rapunzel was banished
deep into the forest.

Still angry, the witch waited until she heard the prince call out,

"Rapunzel, Rapunzel, let down your hair."

Down to the ground tumbled Rapunzel's long, golden hair, and up climbed the prince.

"Ha!" cried the witch, when the prince reached the top. "You've come for Rapunzel, but she has gone and you'll never find her!"

Shocked, the prince ...

f
e
l
l

from the tower, into a thorn bush on the ground. The bush broke his fall, but the thorns scratched his eyes, making him blind.

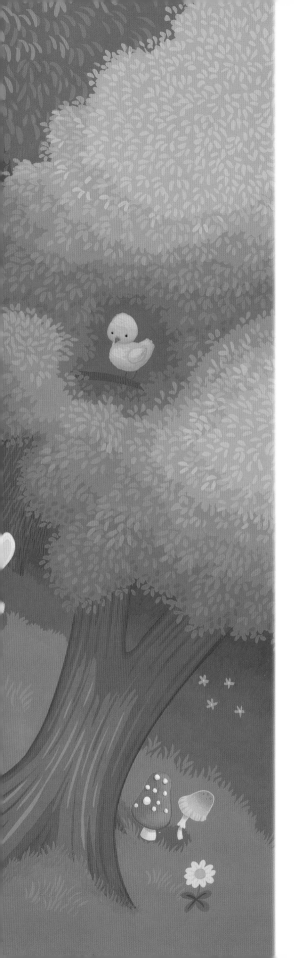

For many months, the blind prince wandered through the wilderness.

One day, he heard someone singing in the woods,

"As I roam from tree to tree, My true love's face I long to see."

"Rapunzel?" he called, "Is that you?"

Rapunzel ran through the woods.

Her tears of joy fell into the prince's eyes and he could see again! Rapunzel had short hair now, but she was just as beautiful as ever.

Rapunzel and the prince traveled the world, visiting all the places Rapunzel had longed to see.

And they never saw the old witch again!

What Should I Wear, Huggle Buggle Bear?

Get set, Huggle Buggle,
Let's all play outside.
We'll run and we'll jump,
We'll swing and we'll slide.

Come on, Huggle Buggle,
Let's get dressed and go!
First underwear, then socks—
Where are they? Oh, no!

I've checked in the laundry
And looked in the drawer.
But there's only one sock
Lying here on the floor.

Lost! Gone!
Where could it be?
I wish Huggle Buggle
Could find it for me.

Silly Rubadub Duck—
You can't wear that.
It's my missing odd sock,
Not a funny duck's hat!

Thanks Huggle Buggle!
You're the best-ever bear.
But I'm still not quite ready—
What else should I wear?

74

What if it's cold
When I whizz down the slide?
I need to be warm
To go playing outside.
I'll wear my green pants—
My favorite pair.

But where's my red sweater?
It was over there.

I must find my sweater
Before I can play.
It was hanging up—
Someone took it away!

Lost! Gone!
Where could it be?
I wish Huggle Buggle
Could find it for me.

76

What a surprise!
It's my friend Ellie Nellie.
My sweater's an apron
Tied around her soft belly!

Thanks Huggle Buggle!
You're the best-ever bear.
But I'm still not quite ready—
What else should I wear?

What if it rains
When I'm swinging up high?
I want to wear something
To keep myself dry.

I'll put on my boots,
While I sit on this stair ...

Now, where is my coat?
Oh no, it's not there!

My coat belongs here,
On its own special hook.
It has to be found,
But where should I look?

Lost! Gone!
Where could it be?
I wish Huggle Buggle
Could find it for me.

My friend Woolly Lamb
Has borrowed my coat.
It's the wavy blue sea
Underneath his toy boat!

Thanks Huggle Buggle!
You're the best-ever bear.
But I'm still not quite ready—
What else should I wear?

What if the wind
Blows the leaves on the ground?
I could wrap up tight
Before running around.

I'll pull on my gloves,
My snuggly hat, too ...

But where is my scarf?
Oh, what should I do?

It must be here somewhere—
It's my red-and-white one!
I saw it just yesterday—
Where has it gone?

Lost! Vanished!
Where could it be?
I wish Huggle Buggle
Could find it for me.

My scarf is a jump rope—
That's very funny!
But who is holding it?
Babbity Bunny!

OK, Huggle Buggle,
What now? Do you know?
If everyone's ready,
It's playtime—LET'S GO!

Five Little Ducks

Five little ducks went swimming one day,
Over the hills and far away.
Mother Duck said, "Quack, quack, quack, quack,"
But only four little ducks came back.

*(Repeat the rhyme, counting down from four little ducks
to one little duck …)*

One little duck went swimming one day,
Over the hills and far away.
Mother Duck said, "Quack, quack, quack, quack,"
And five little ducks came swimming back.

One, Two, Buckle My Shoe

One, two, buckle my shoe,

Three, four, knock on the door,

Five, six, pick up sticks,

Seven, eight, lay them straight,

Nine, ten, a big fat hen,

Eleven, twelve,
    dig and delve,

Thirteen, fourteen,
    maids a-courting,

Fifteen, sixteen,
    maids in the kitchen,

Seventeen, eighteen,
    maids in waiting,

Nineteen, twenty,
    my plate's empty!

Five Little Monkeys

Five little monkeys jumping on the bed,
One fell off and bumped his head.
Mama called the Doctor, and the Doctor said,
"No more monkeys jumping on the bed!"

Four little monkeys jumping on the bed,
One fell off and bumped her head.
Papa called the Doctor, and the Doctor said,
"No more monkeys jumping on the bed!"

*(Repeat the rhyme, counting down from three
little monkeys to one little monkey …)*

One little monkey jumping on the bed,
He fell off and bumped his head.
Mama called the Doctor, and the Doctor said,
"Put those monkeys straight to bed!"

Hickory Dickory Dock

Hickory dickory dock,
The mouse ran up the clock.
The clock struck one,
The mouse ran down,
Hickory dickory dock.

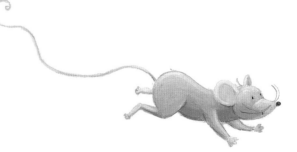

Three Blind Mice

Three blind mice, three blind mice,
See how they run, see how they run!
They all ran after the farmer's wife,
Who cut off their tails with a carving knife,
Did you ever see such a thing in your life
As three blind mice?

One, Two, Three, Four, Five

One, two, three, four, five,
Once I caught a fish alive.
Six, seven, eight, nine, ten,
Then I let it go again.

Why did you let it go?
Because it bit my finger so.
Which finger did it bite?
This little finger on the right.